# Angelical Wisdoms

Messages to nourish the soul

**JULIA VAN DER SLUYS**

Copyright © 2024

All rights reserved. This book or any portion thereof may not be reproduced or used in any manner whatsoever without the express written permission of the author except for the use of brief quotations in a book review.

Printed in Australia
First Printing, 2024
ISBN: 978-1-7636899-7-8
White Light Publishing
www.whitelightuniversal.com.au

# This is your moment...

Your moment to just be with yourself and the Angels

A moment in time just for you...

To feel their calming embrace

To feel the call of your own soul

To select a message
just for you today

To feel that message
to your core and let it
works its magic on you

Allow yourself
this moment.

# How to Use

There is literally no wrong or right way to use this book. It is there for you to use your own little inner nudges on what feels right for YOU.

You may want to flick through and see what grabs your attention.

You may want to read it cover to cover and just let it all sink in.

My favourite way is for you to ask yourself and the Angels what message you need today. Then allow yourself to open to a page and let the words sink in and resonate.

Each time you touch this book, it may work a little differently. Perhaps one day it wants you to journal on the message you receive and dive in a little deeper.

Other days it may just want you to see the message, smile and give thanks and go about your day while it marinates in your soul.

Do what feels right for YOU!

But always allow the juiciness of the Angels messages to penetrate deep into your being and let it works its magical mojo.

Close your eyes and just be for a moment.

Allow your awareness to creep to where your soul resides. See the flame or sparkle that lives there and breathe a little extra pep into it. Say hello to it, embrace it like an old friend and just simply be with your true self for just a spot in time. Feel that joy and peace? That is yours for the taking whenever you want it.

You are so needed on this Planet - right here right now! It is not a coincidence or by chance that you are here. Go forth and sprinkle your unique amazingness out into the world for you have no idea how much of a difference you could truly make. You don't need Tinkerbell's dust when you have your own special brand.

**ALL YOU NEED TO BE IS YOU.** IT DOESN'T MATTER THE JOB YOU HAVE, THE SCHOOLING YOU TOOK. **ALL THAT MATTERS** IS THAT YOU **SPREAD YOUR LOVE AROUND LIKE BUTTER ON BREAD.**

Give love
and thanks
to all parts
of you...

...both seemingly good or bad for they make you into the magnificent creature that you are. It is only you that can give them 'good' or 'bad' roles... so accept them for what they are and just love yourself.

## GO ON WE DARE YOU.

# WHEN YOU FEEL UNFULFILLED

...it is because you are not seeing the abundance and fantasticness that is already right in front of you.

Take a second, to see how truly blessed you really are. It could be a place to live, people to love, food to eat, clean water, the sun on your face. These are the little miracles for you to discover and enjoy each and every single day.

The list is endless and I bet you feel mighty fine now right?

Say it with me...
I am a magnificent person and I deserve the very best this life has to offer. I shine with love, joy and laughter.

# Let your inner child run free...

...even if it is for 3 minutes to dance to a silly song, colour in or blow bubbles!

# EMBRACE THE JOY IN THE SIMPLE THINGS

...the laughter and curiosity that springs forth when your child is out to play.

YOUR INNER CHILD NEEDS TO FEEL LOVED, SAFE AND SPECIAL.

## TAKE THIS MOMENT NOW TO CLOSE YOUR EYES AND CONNECT.

GIVE YOUR LITTLE SELF A BIG BIG HUG AND LET THEM KNOW JUST HOW SAFE AND LOVED THEY TRULY ARE, FOR YOU ARE THE ADULT NOW THAT CAN PROVIDE THIS.

# Shout it from the rooftops...

**... I AM going to have a fabulous day because I CHOOSE to!**
You are the maker of your own destiny so choose a fantabulous one.

## WE LOVE YOU SO VERY MUCH AND ARE ALWAYS STANDING BY YOUR SIDE.

Ask us for guidance, assistance, love and we will gladly provide. We want you to succeed just as much you want to.

You cannot have stars without a dark sky, a rainbow without clouds - the same as your life can not be truly happy without feeling the lows as well to truly remind you how very special your life really is. Just remember the darkness never lasts.

**WHAT DO YOU WANT YOUR LIFE TO LOOK LIKE?** IMAGINE IT, FEEL IT AND IF IT ISN'T HOW YOU WANT IT... ASK YOURSELF WHY? YOU ARE THE RULER IN YOUR KINGDOM SO GO OUT AND GET **WHAT YOU WANT.**

## BEING ABUNDERIFIC -
abundant beyond belief - is a state of mind.

Choose flowers and butterflies in your mind garden rather than weeds and slugs and feel truly rich each and every day.

Stomp it out. Shake that booty. Get all the feelings that are coursing through your body out in a wonderfully creative way. Just be mindfully aware that you are stomping out that anger, shaking away the blues and so it will be.

## LOOK UP AT THE STARS AND SAY A BIG HELLO.

Let one of them choose you to be your guiding light, your pinpoint of light when things get dark and too much. Ask to be shown your friend in the sky.

**Your soul is pure radalicious energy...**

...like the finest wine, the sparkliest diamond, the prettiest picture - that is YOU! All the bestest things wrapped up in one package known as you!!!

## HOW COOL!!!

When you moan and groan, all you do is lower your vibes and attract more of the same. Learn to see the best in all situations and if needed, write out the problem and then take a step back and see it from all angles.

**GO OUTSIDE AND GIVE YOUR WORRIES, LOW VIBRATIONS TO MOTHER EARTH.** SEE THEM SINKING DOWN INTO THE GROUND FROM YOUR FEET. **GIVE LOTS OF LOVE, GRATITUDE & THANKS FOR THIS DELICIOUS GIFT.**

**Being whole and complete means welcoming and hugging every single part of you, every thing that has happened to you, everything that makes you YOU!**

Learn to praise your **dark** as well as your light to live in perfect harmony.

# FORGIVENESS

Forgiveness means you are ready to move past the situation, learn from it and carry on. Forgiveness is something you do for yourself, as it stops you from being stuck in the past, stuck in low vibes and just plain old stuck.

**Give yourself the gift of forgiveness today.**

**Be love.
See love.
Talk love.
Eat love.
Just love
love love.**

# Life happens in a blink of an eye.

Do you want that blink to be full of pain and suffering or do you want joy and pleasures?

# ONLY YOU HAVE THE POWER TO CHOOSE MY DEAR.

**BE YOUR OWN BEST FRIEND, PARENT, LOVER, TEACHER.** THAT WAY YOU WILL ALWAYS HAVE THESE ROLES AT YOUR DISPOSAL AND EVEN BETTER IT SHOWS JUST HOW MUCH YOU LOVE YOURSELF TO BE EVERYTHING YOU COULD POSSIBLY NEED.

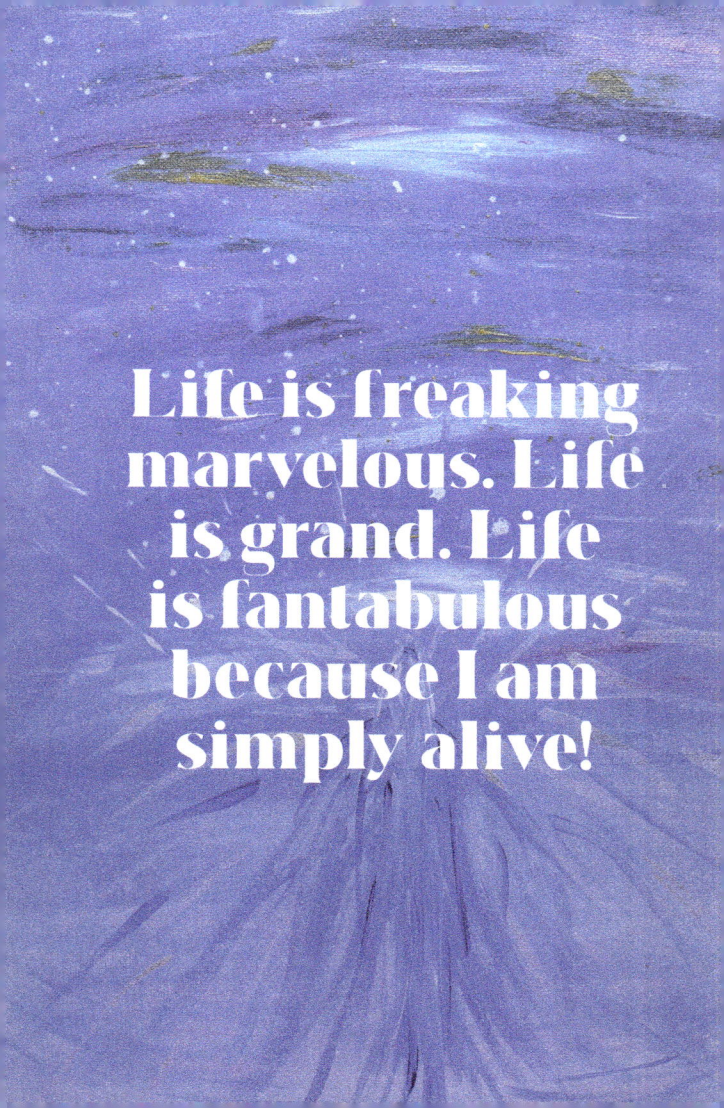

I am everything to me.
The end!

**Give your worries and cares to us.**

See them lift and drain off you and into the universe. Know they are taken care of and we will help guide you. Also know that it is up to you to be an active participant in achieving what you want.

Peace, joy, love, calmness, elation, happiness are all yours for the taking in every moment of your life. You only have to remember this is your God given right to feel these. That it is your souls natural state of being and that all the low vibrations of hurt, anger, worry and sadness are not. So let them go and get back into the flow of your soul.

**ALL THE CHOICES ARE YOURS, YES THEY ARE.** EVEN WHEN YOU CANNOT CONTROL IT - YOUR CHOICE IS TO CONTROL YOUR REACTION TO IT. WHAT CHOICES ARE YOU GOING TO CHOOSE TODAY?

Thoughts use the same amount of energy as if you were actively doing it and your body believes everything that you are thinking. So take a second to make sure you are conserving your energy and giving yourself wonderful things to think on.

## TIME HEALS ALL WOUNDS IT'S TRUE!

Yet so does standing in your power and taking responsibility for what is or has occurred in your life. Be the nurse to your own wounds and watch them heal before your very own eyes.

## WE ARE ALL CHEERING YOU ON EVERY SINGLE DAY.

Imagine your own cheer squad spelling out your name, shaking pom poms just for you and jumping up and down whenever something great happens.

I BELIEVE IN ME BECAUSE **UNDER MY CLOTHES** - I HAVE WONDER WOMAN, SUPERMAN, HULK AND ALL THESE OTHER SUPERHEROES COSTUMES UNDERNEATH. **I SAVE ME.**

I am grateful for everything in my life - the good the bad the beautiful and the ugly.

## IT TAKES ALL KINDS OF PEOPLE TO MAKE UP THIS WORLD.

You're not going to gel with all of them, but what you can do is respect and accept them no matter what. Remember you cannot change a person but you can change YOUR reactions to them. And BOOM world peace can commence!

# Hakuna Matata!!!

### It's a problem free philosophy!
No worries doesn't mean things are going to be carefree and fantastic all the time - it means dealing with the downs as well as you deal with the highs. It's knowing it is only temporary and the perfect moment to practice Hakuna Matata!

**Sometimes the apple cart needs to be shaken, pushed over, stomped on and made into apple juice.**

ACCEPTANCE IS REALISING;
**I AM WHAT I AM
AND I AM**
TOTALLY OK WITH THAT.
I CAN EVOLVE AT ANY TIME
AND AM DOING SO
ON A DAILY BASIS.

## MY LIFE IS LUXURIOUS AND IS EXACTLY AS I CHOOSE TO HAVE IT.

I can make any choices I wish to and do so always.

Love is what gets all your cylinders firing. That lights up your soul.

Love is truly what makes the world go round smoothly.

Look for our signs, look for our love. You will find it in everything if you just care to take a look.

Life can be lemons if we choose to only focus on the lemony parts. It can also be rainbows and butterflies even with the lemons if you choose to see the sparkle, magic and positivity. Let the lemons be part of that gold at the end of the rainbow. The nectar that the butterflies sip from.

**You are eternal,** so don't think you have no time, it is only by thinking you have no time that you do not have any.

Human life is so special, you are capable of so much, get to enjoy nature, have these amazing bodies that mostly function on their own!

# EMBRACE, LOVE EVERYTHING ABOUT THIS LIFE. SEE THE MIRACLES IN BEING HERE.

**I release the need to be angry as I am in charge of my future.**

## ALLOWANCE AND ACCEPTANCE IS WHAT IS NEEDED TO MOVE ON FROM ANYTHING.

Are you going to allow and accept today?
**What is it you can allow and accept to go forward?**

**CHOICE IS SUCH A POWERFUL WORD.**
YOU HAVE THE CHOICE TO THINK/
FEEL/ BE ANY WAY YOU CHOOSE TOO.
**HOW AMAZING IS THAT?!**
WHICH WAY ARE YOU CHOOSING?

SIT WITH YOUR HAND ON YOUR HEART AND **ALLOW THAT LOVE TO RADIATE OUT. FEEL IT WITH EVERY FIBRE OF YOUR BEING. BE THAT LOVE. ALLOW THAT MAGICAL FEELING TO STAY WITH YOU, TO BE PRESENT WITH YOU THROUGHOUT YOUR DAY.**

Upon waking - smile and stretch and say
**YAY to a new day for magic to happen.**

# I ALLOW MY DAY TO BE GUIDED, POSITIVE AND TOTALLY MAGICAL!

Let your journey be meaningful. Don't just exist. Take a step today towards your own version of greatness.

## GO OUT AND GRAB WHAT YOU WANT WITH BOTH HANDS.

Let the fear push you forward, let the excitement propel you to great heights. Use everything to your advantage.

Peace is best felt through the chaos of our lives...

that is when we know we have mastered it, just a little, when we can find it in the hardness of our life and still find a positive,

**STILL FIND A WAY TO SMILE AND SEE THAT LIGHT AT THE END OF THE TUNNEL.**

## REMEMBER TO STOP AND WATCH THOSE CLOUDS GENTLY ROLL BY...

and remember that your life is just like those clouds - sometimes white and fluffy, sometimes dark and foreboding - but they always drift past. It never lasts. Just remember that.

# STOP!!!
RIGHT NOW PUT A BIG SMILE ON YOUR DIAL, THROW YOUR HANDS IN THE AIR AND DO A LITTLE WIG-GLE. MAKES YOU FEEL GOOD HUH? THIS CAN BE DONE AT ANY TIME **TO RESET YOU TO JOY!**

**How can you expect to see the stars without darkness. How can you expect to see a rainbow without sunshine. How can you expect to enjoy your light, without a little darkness and vice versa... embrace them both.**

Being different and unlike any other is what makes us human unique and freaking awesome!

Glide like a bird, slime along like a snail, but most importantly keep going to your destination, to your evolvement. It doesn't matter how you do it. It is whatever is right for only you!

## YOU DON'T NEED TO BE PERFECT, HOW BORING WOULD THAT BE!

You don't need to be exactly like the next person... how boring would that be! Instead you need to embrace you, regardless of what you do or don't do, regardless of what you look like, regardless of anything at all.

TURN THOSE LISTS OF I WISHES INTO I WANTS, I WILL, I HAVE ALREADY! ACT AS IF YOU ALREADY HAVE THEM AND ARE LIVING THEM. MAKE SURE YOUR LIST ISN'T A GRUMBLY MOAN OF YOUR LIFE THOUGH, AND ONLY CHOOSE EVOLVEMENT (CHANGES) OF YOURSELF IF IT ACTUALLY BRINGS YOU MORE IN ALIGNMENT TO SOUL, MORE INTO FINISHING THOSE LIFE LESSONS - NOT BECAUSE YOU FEEL YOU SHOULD BE LIKE SOMEONE ELSE OR BETTER JUST BECAUSE.

Listen to what your body wants and needs to be healthy. Learn to enjoy all food. Do exercise that is right for you. Some people are triathletes and some are not. It is what we tell ourselves is bad, is good, that we should do - that is the problem. Everything in moderation, listening to that voice within that says enjoy that or hmm not that. That is what is right. Ask your crew for help if you need it.

I AM SO FREAKING **WORTHY OF BEING HERE.** EVERYTHING I DO IS BECAUSE I KNOW **I DESERVE TO BE HERE.** BECAUSE I WANT TO BE HERE AND MY BODY IS THE CUP **THAT HOLDS MY SOUL SO I HONOUR IT.**

## IT DOESN'T MATTER IF ANYONE LIKES YOU OR EVEN HATES YOU.

What matters is that you love yourself unconditionally. This starts spreading the goodness to how others treat you, see you and how your life goes. Sure there are always going to be those that still think you suck but there will be more who think you're the bee's knees and hey I'm sure you don't like everyone so it all evens out.

I am one with all. That means that all that power that I don't think I have is all a load of hog wash. How can I not have access to it, when it is part of me?? Time to jump on the power train hey??

## DID YOU KNOW YOUR LIFE IS YOUR OWN?

Imagine you can change anything you want to, be or do anything you want to. You can draw a line in the sand at any moment in time and choose something different. How freaking cool is that?! So the biggest question is... now what are you going to do with that gold nugget of info?

# I LOVE ME.
SHOUT IT FROM THE ROOFTOPS.
ALLOW EVERY ACTION YOU TAKE TO REINFORCE IT.
# BE LOVE.
BE TOTALLY IN LOVE WITH YOURSELF. GIVE YOURSELF COMPLIMENTS. TAKE YOURSELF OUT ON DATES. SPOIL YOUR-SELF.
**JUST BE LOVE.**

You are blooming marvelous. It s as simple as that! Bloom like the flower you are. Whether your petals unfold one at a time  or all at once does not matter. Just allow them to bloom as they are meant to.

You do not have to search for Peace. It has been with you all this time. Just allow it to surface, ask for it, practice it. It doesn't mean that crap doesn't happen to you anymore, but it does mean that you get over it quicker. You celebrate the lessons you learn in everything and can come back to that inner calm much quicker. It is about connecting to your heart space and letting that calm, peace and love to flow to all parts of you, to your aura, to everything you can see and what touches your life.

## LEARN TO WANT TO SEE THE POSITIVES IN EVERYTHING AND THEY WILL SHOW THEM TO YOU.

Raise your vibration by laughing singing and dancing anything that brings a smile to your dial - DO THAT!!! And watch the magic unfold.

Love makes the world go round.
Love makes your soul sing with joy.
Love makes others feel amazing.
Love is pretty rad right? Go sprinkle your
love around. Even sitting there right now,
you can emit your love into the world
to make it a better place.

## WE ARE OUR GENIE.

You can make your wishes come true every single day, if you desire. You probably already are without realising it. Keep your wishes positive - as everything you think and feel has the potential to come true...

**Flick the switch...
Be the light.**

You came here to experience life – not blow through it.

Slow down, relish, enjoy and most importantly feel how amazing each and every day is that you are here on this planet called Earth. Take a moment to appreciate it, what you have, what you have experienced and the lessons learnt from these experiences.

# EVERYTHING IS AN EXTRAORDINARY PART OF YOUR HUMAN EXISTENCE.

I am courageously courageous like a lion. Courageous like a child learning. Courageous like a mouse surviving. I am truly courageous in all of courageousness forms.

## BEING THE CAPTAIN OF YOUR OWN SHIP MEANS TAKING RESPONSIBILITY FOR ALL THE GOOD BAD HAPPY AND SAD THAT HAPPENS TO US.

There are no ifs or buts about it. Make your ship the bomb by repeating after me...
'I am responsible for me and only me.
I say what I let affect me. What I do, how I live my life... That is on me and I choose to make it fantabulous'.

Every day does not have to be profound or extraordinary, they can be ordinary, and sometimes not to pleasant, as it balances out our humanness and makes us appreciate those amazing days. BUT each ordinary day - you yourself can make extraordinary in your own unique way. You do not have to be defined by the ordinariness. You can be the silver lining in your clouds. You can be the beautiful pinks, purples and oranges in a spectacular sunrise. Why you ask? Because you are a part of the Divine that brings these amazing sights to Earth. So you can most definitely bring them into your own life. Don't just let your life be a cloudy existence - bring your own magical moments to them.

TODAY I SHRUG OFF THE WORRY AND DOUBT AS **I TRULY BELIEVE IN DIVINE TIMING. THAT WHAT IS MINE** WILL COME TO ME WHEN IT IS RIGHT TO. I TAKE IMPERFECT ACTION BECAUSE I KNOW THE **TIMING IS ALWAYS RIGHT.** I KNOW I HAVE A PIT CREW AROUND ME ALWAYS ASSISTING AND CARING ABOUT ME... SO THERE IS NO NEED FOR THAT WORRY AND DOUBT I HAVE BEEN WEARING FOR ALL THIS TIME.

WHILE GOING GANGBUSTERS
IS ALL WELL AND GOOD,
A SLOW AND STEADY APPROACH IS ALSO OKAY.
AS YOU ALIGN WITH YOUR SOUL
AND WHO YOU TRULY ARE AND THE UNIVERSE –
YOU CANNOT GO WRONG.
SLOW AND STEADY MEANS SETTING FIRM FOUNDATIONS
THAT ARE GOING TO TRULY LAST.
IT IS CALMLY PUTTING
ONE FOOT IN FRONT OF THE OTHER,
NO MATTER WHAT
IS HAPPENING IN YOUR WORLD.

Take a moment right this very momento - yep right now to appreciate something that has happened to you today, like really feel it in your soul, your toes - with your whole being. Feel the deliciousness of it. It can be the smallest thing to the biggest thing - it simply does not matter. Even something less than pleasant can be appreciated... as when you learn to do that - it takes away the negative connotation and just becomes a fabulous learning experience. Which means YOU are on your way to **Radaliciousness!!! Repeat after me...**

# " I ALIGN WITH MY SOUL AND GO AT A PACE THAT IS PERFECTLY RIGHT FOR ME. "

# Rejoice in living.

Rejoice in feeling. Rejoice in choices.
Just simply Rejoice.

It is so amazing to be alive.

# About Me

Julia is an author, publisher, and the creative heart behind The Giving Deck. Her mission? To help people hit pause, tune into their inner wisdom, and remember that love - starting with yourself - is the real magic of life.

Through her books and playful card decks, she invites you to embrace your messy, beautiful humanity. After all, who said self-discovery couldn't come with a side of laughter?

When not writing or designing, she's wandering in nature with her dogs, chatting with her chooks and duck, or plotting her next chocolate break. Because connection, joy, and a little fresh air make everything better.

www.ingramcontent.com/pod-product-compliance
Lightning Source LLC
Chambersburg PA
CBHW042321090526
44585CB00024BA/2738